RUTH
BADER GINSBURG

JESSIE ALKIRE

Checkerboard
Library

An Imprint of Abdo Publishing
abdobooks.com

ABDOBOOKS.COM

Published by Abdo Publishing, a division of ABDO, PO Box 398166, Minneapolis, Minnesota 55439.
Copyright © 2020 by Abdo Consulting Group, Inc. International copyrights reserved in all countries.
No part of this book may be reproduced in any form without written permission from the publisher.
Checkerboard Library™ is a trademark and logo of Abdo Publishing.

Printed in the United States of America, North Mankato, Minnesota
052019
092019

 THIS BOOK CONTAINS
RECYCLED MATERIALS

Design and Production: Mighty Media, Inc.
Editor: Megan Borgert-Spaniol
Cover Photograph: Shutterstock Images
Interior Photographs: AP Images, pp. 11, 15, 28 (top, bottom right); Fred Schilling/Supreme Court of the
United States/Wikimedia Commons, p. 27; Levan Ramishvili/Flickr, p. 23; Seth Poppel/Yearbook Library,
pp. 9, 28 (bottom left); Shutterstock Images, pp. 17, 19, 25, 29 (top left, top right); Steve Petteway/
Supreme Court of the United States/Wikimedia Commons, pp. 5, 7, 21, 29 (bottom); U.S. Department of
State/Flickr, p. 13

Library of Congress Control Number: 2019934070

Publisher's Cataloging-in-Publication Data
Names: Alkire, Jessie, author.
Title: Ruth Bader Ginsburg / by Jessie Alkire
Description: Minneapolis, Minnesota : Abdo Publishing, 2020 | Series: Checkerboard biographies |
    Includes online resources and index.
Identifiers: ISBN 9781532119941 (lib. bdg.) | ISBN 9781532174803 (ebook)
Subjects: LCSH: Ginsburg, Ruth Bader--Juvenile literature. | United States. Supreme Court--Juvenile
    literature. | Women judges--Biography--Juvenile literature. | Judges--Biography--Juvenile literature.
    | Women's rights--United States--History--20th century--Juvenile literature.
Classification: DDC 347.732634 [B]--dc23

CONTENTS

CHAPTER 1

RBG

Ruth Bader Ginsburg is a famous Supreme Court justice. She was the second woman to serve on the court. She has held her position for more than 25 years.

Ginsburg has been a leading figure in the fight for gender equality. Early in her career, she struggled to find work and faced **discrimination** because of her gender. This experience led Ginsburg to fight for change. Her life's work aimed to ensure that everyone, regardless of gender, would be treated fairly by the law.

Ginsburg is also famous for being outspoken both in court and in politics. Her intelligence and wit have made her an icon. She has been featured in comic books, in movies, on TV shows, and on clothing. With her attitude and humor, Ginsburg is like no other Supreme Court justice before her!

> I try to teach through my opinions, through my speeches, how wrong it is to judge people on the basis of what they look like, color of their skin, whether they're men or women.

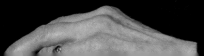

Ginsburg's well-known look includes glasses, a lace collar, and big earrings. Her image has appeared on shirts, posters, and more.

CHAPTER 2

FAMILY VALUES

Joan Ruth Bader was born on March 15, 1933, in New York City, New York. From early childhood, she went by her middle name, Ruth. Her father, Nathan, was a fur manufacturer. Her mother, Celia, stayed at home and helped with her husband's business.

Nathan and Celia were Jewish. Nathan had **immigrated** to the US from Russia as a child. Celia had been born in the US to Austrian immigrant parents. Both Nathan and Celia's families had left Europe to avoid religious **persecution**. They came to the US in search of freedom and better opportunities.

Nathan and Celia taught Ruth to value her Jewish roots. Celia told Ruth about the Jewish value *tikkun olam,* or "world repair." This value taught Ruth to help others through acts of kindness. It became a guiding principle through Ruth's entire life.

EARLY LOSS

Ruth had one older sister, Marilyn. When Marilyn was six, she died from meningitis, an illness that causes swelling in the brain and spine. Ruth was just 14 months old when Marilyn died.

BIO BASICS

NAME: Ruth Bader Ginsburg

NICKNAMES: RBG; **Notorious** R.B.G.

BIRTH: March 15, 1933, New York City, New York

SPOUSE: Martin Ginsburg (1954-2010)

CHILDREN: Jane and James

FAMOUS FOR: her role as Associate Justice on the US Supreme Court; being a leading figure in the gender equality movement

ACHIEVEMENTS: being the second woman appointed to the US Supreme court, a position she has held for more than 25 years; speaking and writing about gender equality around the world; becoming an icon for her attitude and strong beliefs

CHAPTER 3

EXCELLING IN EDUCATION

When Ruth was growing up, women were rarely encouraged to pursue education or careers. Instead, women were expected to get married and raise children. If women did work, it was typically in low-skill positions. And women were paid less than men at the same job.

Ruth's parents wanted more for their daughter. Celia had never attended college. Instead, she had worked to earn money so her brother could go to college. This selfless act taught Ruth to be generous toward others.

> **My mother told me to be a lady. And for her, that meant be your own person, be independent.**

It also taught her to value her education and be independent. Ruth did well in school and received excellent grades.

While Ruth was attending James Madison High School, Celia became ill. She was **diagnosed** with **cancer**. Celia died the day before Ruth's

Ruth received a New York State scholarship to attend Cornell University. A scholarship is money or aid given to help a student continue his or her studies.

graduation. As Ruth faced this loss, she stayed focused on her education. She soon began college at Cornell University in New York.

CHAPTER 4

CAREER CHALLENGES

Ruth did well at Cornell University. She also met fellow student Martin Ginsburg. The two began dating. With Martin's support and the encouragement of her professors, Ruth decided to become a lawyer.

In June 1954, Ruth graduated first in her class with a degree in government. That same month, Ruth and Martin got married. Ruth changed her name to Ruth Bader Ginsburg. Soon after, Martin was **drafted** into the US Army. The couple moved to Oklahoma, where Martin was stationed for two years.

While living in Oklahoma, Ginsburg became pregnant with her first child, Jane. Ginsburg was working at the Social Security Administration. But she was **demoted** when she revealed that she was pregnant. At the time, this kind of **discrimination** was legal.

> **Women will have achieved true equality when men share with them the responsibility of bringing up the next generation.**

Ginsburg and Martin were married for 56 years until Martin's death in 2010. Ginsburg has called Martin one of the key people in her success.

Martin completed his military service in 1956. Then the family settled in Massachusetts. There, both Ginsburg and Martin attended Harvard Law School. Ginsburg juggled school with caring for her daughter. This was uncommon during a time when women were expected to be full-time mothers.

While attending law school, Ginsburg was one of only nine women in a class of more than 500 people. She often felt her male classmates and teachers were hostile and unaccepting because she was a woman. The **dean** of the law school even asked Ginsburg to defend her place in the school. He told her she was taking up a spot that could have otherwise gone to a man.

Ginsburg had to work hard to prove she was just as smart and capable as any man in her class. She soon stood out at Harvard. She even served on the staff of the *Harvard Law Review*. This student-run law journal had historically been produced mostly by men.

Meanwhile, Ginsburg and her husband received difficult news. Martin was **diagnosed** with **cancer** in 1957. While Martin fought the illness, Ginsburg was his caregiver. She also helped him with his schoolwork in addition to doing her own.

Like Ginsburg, former Secretary of State Hillary Clinton had attended law school. Ginsburg believed Clinton faced unfair criticism as a 2016 presidential candidate because she was a woman.

Martin recovered and graduated from Harvard. He was soon offered a job at a law firm in New York City. The family moved to New York, and Ginsburg transferred to Columbia Law School. In 1959, she graduated at the top of her class.

CHAPTER 5

SLOW BUT STEADY SUCCESS

Despite her rank in law school, Ginsburg struggled to find a job. At the time, very few women were lawyers. Few law firms considered women, especially mothers, as serious professionals.

In 1959, Ginsburg got a job as a **law clerk**. Then in 1961, she returned to Columbia to work on an international research project. For this role, Ginsburg traveled to Sweden to study the country's legal system. She later published a book about this research.

In 1963, Ginsburg was hired as an assistant professor at Rutgers Law School in New Jersey. However, Ginsburg had to accept a lower salary than male teachers at the school. Her boss told her this was because she had a husband to support her.

Ginsburg feared further **discrimination** when she became pregnant with her second child. Ginsburg remembered being **demoted** when she was pregnant

Jane Ginsburg would eventually become a law professor like her mother. James Ginsburg (*to right of Ginsburg*) would become a music producer.

with Jane. So this time, she wore loose clothing to hide her growing belly. She waited to announce her pregnancy until her teaching contract was renewed for another year.

Ginsburg and Martin welcomed their son, James, in 1965. Ginsburg continued to teach at Rutgers for several years. In 1969, she was promoted to professor.

CHAPTER 6

THE FIGHT FOR EQUALITY

Ginsburg's experiences of **discrimination** inspired her life's work. In the years following her promotion, she became a leader in the fight for gender equality. In 1970, she co-founded the *Women's Rights Law Reporter*. This was the first US law journal focused on gender equality.

In 1972, Ginsburg co-founded the Women's Rights Project at the American Civil Liberties Union (ACLU). She served as a lawyer for the organization, taking on cases of sex discrimination. She argued that such discrimination **violates** the US Constitution.

Ginsburg also left Rutgers in 1972. From there, she returned to Columbia Law School, this time as a professor.

FIRST CASE

In Ginsburg's first **oral argument** before the Supreme Court, she fought for servicewoman Sharron Frontiero. The US Air Force had denied Frontiero benefits for her husband, whom she supported. Ginsburg said this was unfair because servicemen were granted benefits for their wives.

From 2004 to 2011, *Forbes* magazine named Ginsburg one of the World's 100 Most Powerful Women.

While teaching, Ginsburg continued to pursue cases of sex **discrimination**. In 1973, she argued and won her first case before the US Supreme Court. She went on to argue in five more Supreme Court cases in the 1970s. She won four of the five.

CHAPTER 7

FROM LAWYER TO JUDGE

Ginsburg became a rising star in the fight for gender equality in the 1970s. She proved that **discrimination** would not hold her back. Ginsburg reached a new level of success in 1980. That year, President Jimmy Carter appointed her to the US **Court of Appeals** for the District of Columbia Circuit. Ginsburg was now a judge!

As a judge, Ginsburg became known for her **logical** approach to the law. She believed all people should be treated the same and held to the same standards.

Ginsburg served on the court of appeals until 1993. That year, President Bill Clinton nominated her as Associate Justice for the US Supreme Court. The US Senate then voted Ginsburg onto the court. Ginsburg was sworn in on August 3, 1993. She was only the second woman to serve on the US Supreme Court.

PROMPT & PUNCTUAL

Until January 2019, Ginsburg didn't miss a single day of **oral arguments** in her time on the Supreme Court.

President Bill Clinton watches as newly appointed Supreme Court Justice Ginsburg speaks to the press.

CHAPTER 8

THE HIGHEST COURT

Ginsburg's judicial reputation followed her onto the **Supreme Court.** Many of her career achievements were cases related to gender equality. One such case was *United States v. Virginia* in 1996.

In this case, a military school in Virginia was refusing to admit women. The school argued that its military-based program was unsuitable for women. The Supreme Court decided it was illegal for the school to deny individuals based on gender alone.

Ginsburg delivered the court's **majority opinion.** She noted that the school's program was unsuitable for many people, regardless of gender. She concluded that the school could not turn away qualified students based on general assumptions about gender.

In 1999, Ginsburg received the Thurgood Marshall Award. This honor is awarded to people

POLITICS ASIDE

Ginsburg was known for befriending fellow justices with political views different from her own. One of these friends was Sandra Day O'Connor, the first woman on the Supreme Court.

By 2019, only four women had served on the US Supreme Court. In addition to Ginsburg, they were Sandra Day O'Connor (*left*), Sonia Sotomayor (*middle*), and Elena Kagan (*right*).

in the legal profession who advance civil and human rights. And in 2002, Ginsburg was admitted into the National Women's Hall of Fame!

CHAPTER 9

NOTORIOUS R.B.G.

While Ginsburg was an important figure throughout the 1990s, her fame skyrocketed in the 2000s. In 2000, the Supreme Court ruled in the case *Bush v. Gore*. George W. Bush and Al Gore were candidates in the 2000 presidential election. The race had been so close that Gore wanted a recount of votes in Florida.

In December, the Supreme Court's **majority opinion** decided against the recount of votes. Because of this decision, Bush won the presidency. But Ginsburg disagreed with this decision.

When voting against the majority opinion, Ginsburg said, "I **dissent**." The traditional phrase Supreme Court justices used was, "I respectfully dissent." But Ginsburg considered this an unnecessary and outdated detail.

> " My dissenting opinions . . . are intended to persuade. And sometimes one must be forceful about saying how wrong the court's decision is. "

Ginsburg and Justice Antonin Scalia had opposing views of the US Constitution and the role of the Supreme Court. Yet, Ginsburg and Scalia were known to be good friends.

Ginsburg's forthright **dissent** was noted in accounts of the *Bush v. Gore* decision. She continued to deliver strong dissents in the following years. Because many justices were more conservative than Ginsburg, she often disagreed with the court's **majority opinion**.

People around the nation took note of Ginsburg's direct nature. In 2013, a law student created a blog called "**Notorious** R.B.G." The blog was inspired by Ginsburg's **dissents**. Its title was a play on the name of famous rapper Notorious B.I.G.

Notorious R.B.G. went **viral**. Soon, Ginsburg was widely known by this nickname, or RBG for short. She became famous unlike any other Supreme Court justice in history.

Ginsburg wasn't only famous for her dissents. She was also known for influencing **majority opinions**. In June 2015, the Supreme Court made same-sex marriage legal nationwide. Leading up to this decision, opponents argued same-sex marriage went against tradition. But Ginsburg responded that states shouldn't be allowed to cling to outdated ideas.

Ginsburg's **logical** and firmly stated opinions won the hearts of many Americans. She and her life story became a popular topic of discussion on TV shows, podcasts, and other popular media. And in May 2018, a **documentary** called *RBG* was

LOVE IS LOVE

In 2013, Ginsburg became the first Supreme Court justice to perform the ceremony for a same-sex wedding.

Actress Felicity Jones played Ginsburg in *On the Basis of Sex*.

released. Ginsburg's story played in movie theaters across the nation!

RBG was soon followed by a feature film, *On the Basis of Sex*. Released at the end of 2018, the movie was about Ginsburg's education and early career. Ginsburg even made an appearance at the end of the film! By 2019, it was clear that Ginsburg had made her mark on the world forever.

CHAPTER 10

A REMARKABLE LEGACY

With the release of *RBG* and *On the Basis of Sex*, **Ginsburg gained even more fans.** Her admirers hoped the 85-year-old justice would stay strong and healthy enough to continue serving. Fans of Ginsburg received a scare in November 2018, when Ginsburg fell and broke three ribs. During tests at the hospital, doctors discovered she had lung **cancer**.

Ginsburg had quietly battled cancer twice before in her career. The world waited to see if Ginsburg would recover a third time. In December 2018, Ginsburg had surgery to remove the cancer. Soon after, she was well enough to return to work. She had beaten cancer again!

At the start of 2019, Ginsburg was the oldest justice on the Supreme Court. She had served for more than 25 years. In that time, Ginsburg had participated in

> **Fight for the things that you care about, but do it in a way that will lead others to join you.**

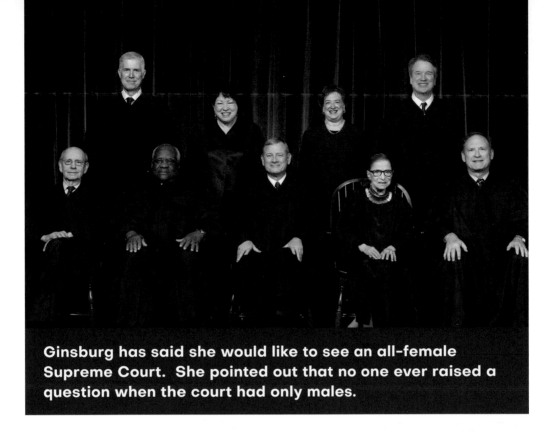

Ginsburg has said she would like to see an all-female Supreme Court. She pointed out that no one ever raised a question when the court had only males.

countless important cases. Her work in service of gender equality had made positive change in the lives of women and men alike.

Despite health concerns, Ginsburg had no plans to retire. She said she would continue to work for as long as she could. However long Ginsburg remained on the court, she had accomplished something remarkable. Her fiery spirit would inspire people long after her career on the Supreme Court concluded.

TIMELINE

1933

Joan Ruth Bader is born in New York City, New York, on March 15.

1959

Ginsburg graduates from Columbia Law School and begins working as a law clerk.

1954

Bader graduates first in her class from Cornell University. She soon marries Martin Ginsburg.

1963

Ginsburg is hired as a law professor at Rutgers Law School.

1970s

Ginsburg becomes a leading figure in the gender equality movement. She argues in six Supreme Court cases and wins five of them.

1993

Ginsburg is nominated and sworn in as Associate Justice on the US Supreme Court.

2018

A documentary, *RBG*, and feature film, *On the Basis of Sex*, about Ginsburg are released in theaters.

1980

Ginsburg is appointed to the US Court of Appeals for the District of Columbia Circuit.

2000

Ginsburg responds, "I dissent," in the Supreme Court case *Bush v. Gore*. This response earns Ginsburg admirers across the nation.

GLOSSARY

cancer—any of a group of often deadly diseases marked by harmful changes in the normal growth of cells. Cancer can spread and destroy healthy tissues and organs.

court of appeals—a court that examines the decisions of lower courts and decides if they were correct.

dean—a person at a college or university who is in charge of guiding students.

demote—to change a person's rank or position to a less important one.

diagnose—to recognize something, such as a disease, by signs, symptoms, or tests.

discrimination (dihs-krih-muh-NAY-shuhn)—unfair treatment, often based on race, religion, or gender.

dissent—to have a different opinion.

documentary—a film that artistically presents facts, often about an event or a person.

draft—to select for required military service.

immigrate—to enter another country to live. Someone who immigrates is called an immigrant.

law clerk—a worker who assists a judge with research, writing, and other legal work.

logical—informed by logic, the science dealing with rules of correct reasoning and proof by reasoning.

majority opinion—a judicial opinion that is shared by more than half the members of a court.

notorious—having a widely known reputation.

oral argument—a spoken argument presented by a lawyer or party involved in a court case.

persecution—the act of treating someone badly. Persecution is based on a person's origin, religion, or beliefs.

violate—to break or ignore a law, rule, or basic right.

viral—quickly or widely spread, usually by electronic communication.

ONLINE RESOURCES

Booklinks
NONFICTION NETWORK
FREE! ONLINE NONFICTION RESOURCES

To learn more about Ruth Bader Ginsburg, please visit **abdobooklinks.com** or scan this QR code. These links are routinely monitored and updated to provide the most current information available.

INDEX